I REME1

By Judy Sutherland

Hello, I'm Brillo

Judy Sutherland © Copyright 2006

All rights reserved

No parts of this publication may be reproduced,
stored in a retrieval system, or transmitted in any
form or by any means, electronic, mechanical,
photocopying, recording or otherwise without the
prior permission of the copyright owner.

British Library Cataloguing In Publication Data
A Record of this Publication is available
from the British Library

ISBN 1846851122
978-1-84685-112-4

First Published March 2006 by

Exposure Publishing, an imprint of Diggory Press,
Three Rivers, Minions, Liskeard, Cornwall,
PL14 5LE, UK
WWW.DIGGORYPRESS.COM

WITH THANKS to my husband for his continuing love, care and support since my illness was diagnosed and for helping me to prepare this book for Publication.

ALL Royalties will be donated to Leukaemia Research.

INDEX

PREFACE

You see I was chosen, yes, I mean actually chosen from a litter of eight other puppies to enlighten and enrich the lives of my new owners. It was an enormous responsibility which, I undertook seriously enough to make a determined effort not to disappoint them.

It wasn't always possible to lay on my bed each night content in the knowledge that, at least in some small way, I had contributed to the lives of my family, but at least I did my best to achieve this. So, if I was more than they had bargained for, they really do only have themselves to blame.

Chapter 1

I THINK almost everyone one who had the dubious honour of being introduced to Brillo, during his action packed fourteen and a half years, will hold some memory, not necessarily fond, firmly embedded in their mind. Such was his great character that on meeting a past acquaintance, sooner or later during the course of conversation they would ask, "Have you still got Brillo?" This question would nearly always be followed by "I remember when...." and some vivid account of one of his usually amusing and sometimes amazing antics would be related in great detail. As many as can be recalled are now included in this true tale of a terrible terrier.

My husband worked long hours and was often away on business, I had just given up work and with time on my hands it seemed an ideal opportunity to buy a puppy to keep me company. Little did we know at that time, we were very soon about to be "owned" by one. We both agreed on a large dog, I adored boxers but this personal preference was quickly overridden when someone told my husband they were terribly boisterous and never really grew up.

Well in hindsight, whoever said that, obviously had no experience of Airedale Terriers, the breed of his choice. Known as the King of Terriers they certainly have an air of calm superiority about them. Together with the fact that Airedales do not moult must be a major factor in their favour, particularly if you prefer your clothes, carpets, and lounge suite to retain their own identity and not be permanently disguised as the family pet.

Quite by chance some well-meaning relatives just happened to know of nine puppies requiring good homes. The litter was just four weeks old and belonged to a couple who ran a small village Post Office in Suffolk. One warm sunny day in July we eagerly made an appointment to view. Never having seen an Airedale puppy before, we were clearly surprised to find that they bear little resemblance to the adult version. They have short stubby legs with extremely knobbly knees, trimmed with huge, almost circular paws that are tan in colour in contrast to their almost totally black body. Mischievous beady, dark brown eyes set deep in their head, peer at you from their jet-black faces just spiked with tan around their little snub noses. As they develop, it is as if they grow out of their little black overcoats, a long square-nosed tan head and long tan legs emerge and they are left with a slender back, cloaked in no more than a sleek black waistcoat.

Meet Candy, my real Mum

Some from the litter were already sold, we preferred to have a male puppy and three were left. I must confess a deliberate effort on my part was secretly being made to select the most mischievous. It was very difficult, they all looked alike, each one a cute little bundle of fun as they rough and tumbled over one another under the watchful eye of Candy their mother, a fine example of the breed. Having hopefully made a successful choice our puppy had his tail dabbed with green paint to ensure we collected the correct one when he was old enough to be weaned.

The name "Brillo" we thought completely epitomized this little urchin whose coarse, wiry coat distinctly resembled a scouring pad. Being on holiday when the other puppies went to their respective new homes, Brillo had the benefit of two extra weeks alone with Candy. Whatever she taught him during those days of individual maternal nurturing and care obviously made him feel very special and was to set him in good stead for the rest of his very eventful life.

It was late August when we finally went to collect Brillo he had almost doubled in size since our first meeting and was a very strong and healthy puppy. We felt extremely mean taking away Candy's last offspring but our new cheeky little baby didn't appear at all perturbed, indeed why should he? There were so many adventures he had to fulfil in his years ahead and plenty of surprises in store for us. His pedigree contained some very elite names in the Airedale world and he was also registered with the Kennel Club under the grand name of "Regimental Legionnaire". We collected his documents together with detailed feeding instructions and waved good-bye to his breeder.

On the journey home Brillo was a very good boy, obviously he had never been in a car before but its soothing motion, together with the warmth and comfort of my lap as he snuggled down into it, soon made him fall fast asleep. The route took us close to my sister's house, convinced she and her family would find him simply adorable we parked the car, carefully avoiding a child's bicycle which happened to be strewn across the driveway. Before we had the opportunity to formally introduce him, Brillo spotted this strange looking contraption as he leaped from the car. He bounded towards it overcome with inquisitive curiosity and was promptly consumed by an overwhelming desire to discover if cycle tyres really were as appetizing as they first appeared. There was no time to divert his attention before his tiny needle-like teeth pierced the rubber and Brillo's startled retreat in response to the hissing of pressurized air caused much amusement to everyone except the owner of the unfortunate bicycle.

Following an apologetic introduction and embarrassing start to his career it seemed expedient for our visit to be kept fairly brief. We took him home to our small house with a tiny garden situated in a fairly hilly part of Essex. Perhaps Brillo's own account of his many other escapades may just possibly make them more acceptable.

Chapter 2

ARRIVING home about mid-afternoon, my new Mum installed me in a well-padded wicker basket placed under one of the work surfaces in the tiny kitchen. To my delight I found there were several other rooms to explore each containing numerous weird objects for me to inspect. I particularly liked the look of the small securely fenced garden where I could play with the numerous toys I had been given, and maybe sample some of the plants.

I knew at this early stage that I was going to be very happy living here, I also knew I was irresistible and so desperately sought attention, that approval became immaterial. Fortunately I didn't have to wait too long before I embarked on this life-long commitment. Some visitors arrived that very evening, obviously I felt obliged to provide the cabaret but soon found entertaining was a very thirsty business and was eternally grateful to the kind lady who kept leaving her drink, in a sparkling cut-glass tumbler, on the floor beside her chair. It looked like water but tasted quite unlike any I had ever lapped before, enhanced with gin I believe, and fizzie bubbles that made me sneeze and everyone else laugh. I made countless efforts to procure the bow-tie one gentleman was wearing but without success and that same evening I also discovered the delicious contents of ashtrays, once initiated I became addicted to these appropriately named dog-ends but sadly the availability of this delicacy was restricted to only certain visitors.

After all the excitement and activity of my day, that first night shut in the kitchen all by myself, I suddenly felt abandoned, afraid and very, very lonely, I began to cry and whimper pitifully. Being so tiny my large basket, although padded with clean fluffy blankets, seemed so cold and bare and there was no Candy and no familiar smells to comfort me. Sheets of newspaper had been scattered on the floor, it was fun at first, ripping those to shreds but my new Mum kept on coming down, not to play with me as I had hoped, but to coax me back to my bed. I did have a few toys in there but they were not very good sport in the middle of the night, especially when there was nobody to impress. Feeling very sorry for myself I continued to cry and potter around until exhaustion eventually prevailed over my misery and I became dead to the world for just a few hours.

I was awake bright and early the next morning, there was bound to be plenty to do. Breakfast of cereal with warm milk kept me sustained until my other meals which were frequent and consisted of small portions of the very best quality mince, there was a rumour the rest of the family sufficed on an inferior grade!

That morning we went visiting again, this time to meet my new Grandparents. Obviously they both thought I was delightful, even though I took a particular liking to a line of tomato plants which, before my visit were smartly standing to attention in a corner of their large garden, I persisted in lying on them despite repeated efforts to remove me. I went visiting often in the first few weeks, but as my course of inoculations was not yet complete, I had to be carried everywhere or taken in the car which I enjoyed immensely. It was far preferable to being left at home on my own which I did not enjoy, but nevertheless had to be done for a short while each day as an essential part of my education, or so I was told.

I quickly learnt that night was a time for sleeping. A busy puppy needs plenty of rest and growing time, besides although I hated to admit it, by the end of each day the thought of curling up in my now cosy basket, which incidentally seemed to be shrinking rapidly, certainly appealed to my weary little body. I'm proud to announce I was fully house trained following three weeks of very strict discipline. I had found it very degrading being constantly supervised, followed everywhere by a bottle of soda water and kitchen roll, used to mop up my little accidents, which I have to confess were sometimes used as a deliberate form of punishment for my Mum when she scolded me. To retaliate I would run and hide under the sideboard to deposit a little puddle as I gazed defiantly up at her.

Growing rapidly, I intended to one day achieve my newest ambition of climbing the stairs which came down into our lounge. So far they had defeated me, I barked at them frantically not that it did much good, and frequently tackled them earnestly but each time I clumsily mastered one yet another loomed up. To a small chap like me it was not dissimilar to mountaineering in my own living room. Despite numerous tumbles, many hours were absorbed with this conquest in mind and of course when I eventually succeeded, a whole new play area was revealed.

When an elderly aunt came to stay later that summer I was on great form. I had a special affinity with her as I discovered she once had the privilege of owning a dog just like me. I always think first impressions are so important and accordingly performed a full and varied display of puppy antics solely for her benefit. I especially enjoyed the afternoon tea we had in the garden when I took advantage of the flat canvas sun-bed it was laid with plates of assorted cakes and cups filled with tea standing in delicate saucers. I used it as a trampoline you see, the crockery made such an unusual tinkling sound as it bounced up and down, tea slopped around in the saucers and several other places as well, as you can imagine, and cakes scattered in all directions. Aunty Dorothy laughed and laughed until tears were running down her cheeks, oh dear, I was in such trouble! My Mum was not quite so amused, she angrily chased me off and I bolted round and round my tiny garden. With my tail firmly clamped between my legs, ears flapping and a fixed mocking expression on my face, I was safe in the knowledge that nobody could possibly catch me, I was going far too fast.

Life was such fun in those early days and I made many new friends. In particular my Mum's special friend Thelma, who was later to assume, what would be considered in human terms, God-parental responsibilities, she would kindly call round to feed me and let me into the garden any time my family went out for the day.

She had a much loved old Labrador called Soames who I admired greatly, he was a glowing example of a well trained dog and patiently tried to teach me to behave. He was exceptionally tolerant when I chewed his ears and ran under his tummy as I incessantly pestered him to play with me, but he never got angry. Walks with Soames were always fun especially across the fields where I was allowed off my lead, Soames was very grown-up and never seemed to need one even when walking on the highways. I remember one day, bored by my ceaseless capers, he went off without me, I was so hurt I faked a bad paw and lay whimpering in the grass. However, once a fair quota of attention had been duly rendered by my Mum and Aunty Thelma, I seemed to make a remarkable recovery and bounded off to be re-united with my big canine friend.

Back home another day, Aunty Thelma watched as my Mum wielded the vacuum cleaner around the dining room, someone had been in there with muddy paws! In her effort she accidentally disturbed an enormous spider which immediately darted for cover. Mistakenly thinking it was in need of rescue, I made a heroic chase, captured the poor innocent creature and playfully tossed it in the air several times until sadly its dismembered remains also needed to be swallowed up by that greedy vacuum cleaner.

Inoculations completed, walks became a frequent and pleasurable pastime. Regularly being taken out three times a day also served to keep my Mum well exercised. There were parks and playing fields that needed to be explored, other dogs to meet and plenty of admirers. I enjoyed most of all walking the footpath across the local golf course and delighted in splashing about in a stream that ran parallel to the path on parts of the course. Obviously there were plenty of trees in need of some gentle watering and birds to chase, not to mention a few rabbits early in the morning. An additional bonus was the occasional golf ball that miraculously appeared to land from nowhere at all, well, what normal active and inquisitive puppy could possibly resist such sport? However the average serious minded owner of the stray golf ball was generally not amused when I playfully ran off with it, I didn't understand that golf is like a religion to some people! My Mum, hiding a smile, would apologize profusely on my behalf, as she persuaded me to surrender my new found toy, prizing open my tiny jaws she returned the precious, but now rather slimy ball to it's disgruntled owner. Sometimes we would take my own toys or brightly coloured bouncy balls with us but as I was frequently distracted and my ability to concentrate was next to none, I invariably forgot where I'd left them in the long grass and the supply soon ran out.

Can I play?

Walks to the shops proved to be another entertaining expedition especially when they involved collecting my large weekly marrowbone from the Butcher's Shop. My personal challenge was to see if I could help it to escape from its carrier bag before we actually reached home, whilst my Mum struggled to keep me under control and successfully carry the rest of the shopping. The walk home was a steep uphill climb, on arriving safely I was encouraged to take my bone into the garden rather than into the lounge. Extracting the marrow and gnawing at the knuckle kept me amused for hours. Sometimes I would dig a large trench in the flower boarder and bury it to enhance the flavour for a further session on another day. I was really gentle and never possessive, anyone could take my bone from me without fear of losing a hand or even a growl.

Chapter 3

SLOWLY the house and garden somehow seemed to be shrinking or maybe I was getting bigger, but fortunately my family had already decided to move. On the whole I was not a destructive puppy, but just when the house was about to be sold I set about gnawing the garden fence in several places which caused a certain amount of displeasure. I wasn't too popular either when I selected one of my Mum's new sandals to re-design the heel. Oh! I nearly forgot to mention, the leg of the kitchen table which received some unappreciated attention one day when I considered I had been left alone for long enough, there was little else on offer to relieve my boredom so this passed the time nicely.

This table was eventually replaced with one that happened to have horizontal panels supporting the underside of the flat tabletop, these conveniently coincided with the exact height of my back and I soon discovered I could obtain sheer ecstasy by gently rocking back and forth against them. Imagine her astonishment when one day, not knowing I was under the table, a surprised lady visitor quietly sipping a cup of tea thought she was involved in séance as the table suddenly began to rhythmically vibrate.

I was six months old when it was deemed necessary to send me on a dog-training course, it was inevitable that I would soon become a very large strong fellow and even at that early stage my determined nature was very much in evidence. My family arranged to send me to Boarding School for two weeks, but as my Mum didn't really want to part with me, she desperately tried to teach me as much as possible beforehand to make my stay easier. I quickly learned to obey the "sit", "stay", and "come" commands within my home environment. Unfortunately, this new found obedience was not very apparent when enjoying the freedom of open spaces but one had to make allowances for my very limited attention span. There was a whole new wide world for me to discover and I was surrounded by so many fascinating distractions, each requiring immediate investigation.

With all the basic groundwork completed, the appointed day came and Mum's star pupil was transported to the training kennels. Nobody was allowed to visit me during the stay for fear of hindering my progress but I'm told regular telephone contact was made. Two weeks later it was explained that a further week would be advisable to perfect my manners, so reluctantly my Mum had to agree.

Finally the day scheduled for collection dawned, my Mum and Dad were taken, unbeknown to me, to a viewing shed where they waited patiently in anticipation of a "newly reformed character" performing a stunning display of obedience tests. I impressively appeared briskly walking to heel beside my Trainer who then attempted to put me through my paces, but sadly the demonstration deteriorated at that point, I managed to confuse even the simplest of commands, proving my three weeks of intensive training to be a complete disaster. Arrogantly unapologetic, my Trainer insisted I was just having an "off day", he adamantly refused to admit his failure to master my wilful and rebellious nature, my Mum and Dad were certainly stunned. Whilst not holding the kennels responsible for my defiant personality, they were extremely angry this had not been recognized sooner and felt they had been grossly misled when agreeing to that additional week. My unrepentant attitude towards the whole fruitless and very expensive fiasco was made even worse when, I now associated any car journey with those horrid kennels and would bark continuously until the homeward run, prior to that my behaviour in the car had always been exemplary.

By the following spring I was almost fully-grown and began to resemble a true Airedale Terrier but my thick wiry coat had grown long and bushy. Actually someone had the cheek to describe me as looking like a reject teddy bear from a very large and famous toyshop in London. My first haircut was an experience to be long remembered by all present. A very nice lady called Anne came to the house with a large brown case, containing a variety of fascinating instruments. The ensuing entertainment lasted several hours as I had been given a bath the previous day and felt even more frisky than usual. Confined to the tiny kitchen floor, Anne patiently clipped and trimmed my coat, manicured my toenails and cleaned my teeth whilst my Mum, despite my playful protests, relentlessly persevered at holding me still. Although there was a thick carpet of discarded fur everywhere I emerged from their combined effort transformed into a magnificent example of my breed. Elegant deep tan legs, smooth jet-black back tapering into a curved tail shaped rather like an umbrella handle, and a bump between my silky envelope shaped ears which Anne kindly described as my "dome of wisdom," and who am I to argue with that? I apparently reminded them of the life size toy dogs, set on wheels with a handle at the back which children used years ago when learning to walk. Without wishing to sound too vain I had indeed developed and been transformed into a remarkably handsome dog.

Is beauty only in the eye of the beholder?

For some extraordinary reason this opinion was not shared by the judge I confronted at my first and only dog show. Even though behaviour was not relevant to his choice for a place in the class, he still failed to recognize my outstanding good looks and conformation. Had my Mum been lying to me I wondered or is beauty only in the eye of the beholder? Actually, being a fairly unusual breed, at least in our part of the country, I was rarely short of unprofessional admirers. Complete strangers would often stop to ask about me and on one such occasion a kindly gentleman actually invited me to meet his equally attractive lady Airedale, but alas, the offer came too late for me and regretfully the canine world was spared a further litter of baby Brillos.

I was trimmed about four times a year thereafter, the task was never easy on account of my playful behaviour but fortunately for Anne there was not an ounce of vice in me and I soon became her favourite Airedale client, whilst she became a very good family friend. There was a short period in my life however when Anne was not available. My Mum, who wouldn't hear of allowing me to go to a grooming parlour, found a very strange lady who was prepared to visit me at home. She actually expected me to stand motionless on a special table she brought with her, anchored to the table was a pole to which I was attached by a noose placed around my neck. Well as you can imagine, I took a very dim view of that, it was no fun at all. On one occasion, my Mum popped out for only a few minutes, when she returned she was horrified to find me hanging from the noose in a rather frantic state. I had somehow fallen off the table you see and was wriggling so much the lady seemed incapable of lifting, unaided, a five stone distraught and panicking mass. I never saw her again thank-goodness and fortunately Anne was able to resume the subsequent clipping sessions.

Over the years I did improve considerably, eventually resigned to the whole boring process, I would lay sprawled across the floor leaving them to it. They would roll me over when necessary and move me around like an old floor mop. When finished feeling fresh and rejuvenated, there was an important ritual to perform, grabbing a shoe, slipper or anything else I could find, I'd rush into the garden to hide or bury it then dash excitedly back indoors to collect my reward for being such a good boy. This was usually a Bonio biscuit which demanded to be chased and tossed about to improve its flavour as I skidded amongst the discarded fur, obviously this activity was a tremendous help to Anne and my Mum, who were still endeavouring to clear up the mess. They were impressed however, that I managed to maintain these antics well into in my advancing years.

Chapter 4

I WAS nearly a year old when we finally moved into a larger house. There was half an acre of garden and my first task was to scrutinize every inch of the boundary, whereupon I successfully managed to detect a few weak areas through which I could broaden my horizons. Sadly for me however, these adventures were soon curtailed when all the fences were securely reinforced. At the end of the garden I discovered a large wooden kennel, I didn't actually live in it but it was fun burying myself under the thick bed of straw if I was shut out of the house for too long when the weather was inclement. My Grandad manufactured a special nameplate for me and erected it above the entrance it was of course called "Brillo's Pad".

My character was developing rapidly, some described my strong determined nature as pure stubbornness but it was always accompanied by my insatiable sense of humour. I never bore any malice even when punished, as I was frequently for some wrong doing, but one of my rather superior and discerning looks cast through my beady eyes was generally enough to mock the entire human race. Indicative of my happy disposition my tail was always held high and wagged merrily from side to side though occasionally, for reasons best kept to myself, it adopted a comical circular action.

I became known as "Wagalot" to many of my acquaintances and "Thunderpaws" was another nickname I acquired, probably from my early morning visitations to assess the consciousness of the recumbent bodies occupying the bed. If the sound of me thundering up the stairs and barging open the bedroom door hadn't already aroused them, staring closely into their faces usually did the trick. Any response, I interpreted as an invitation to leap upon the bed and thereby proceeded to romp around like a hooligan until accompanied back to the kitchen for my breakfast of milk and Bonio biscuits. I then pretended these were extremely viscous, they had to be approached with caution, barked and growled at, pawed and tossed into the air several times to ensure they were completely lifeless before being devoured to the very last crumb. Somehow instinct told me that humans did not appreciate this type of early morning activity when their eyes remained tightly shut. If my staring tactics were unsuccessful, although disenchanted, I would then have the decency to return to my own bed down in the kitchen, albeit not very quietly, and patiently wait for my family to appear in due course. My thunderpaw technique, I also employed when stalking the rabbits and birds that I found trespassing on my lawn, this was obviously of enormous benefit to my prey and I think I achieved a grand score of nil throughout my many years of pursuit.

My Special Kennel

I loved my huge new garden, there was a large rectangular lawn surrounded on three

35

sides by wide, well-stocked flower beds, it was springtime when we moved and before I became addicted to beheading them the daffodils were quite prolific. Gardening was almost a full time job but my own contribution brought much outcry, nobody seemed to appreciate the effort entailed in digging out numerous deep excavations, which I did at least restrict to the flower boarders and not the fine Cumberland turf lawn. Most of these were for burying my marrowbones but others were just for fun and made gardening a bit hazardous when my Mum often stepped backwards into one of them. I created a splendid running track around the garden perimeter. Regular attempts to cultivate this area soon became pointless and readily abandoned once it became so well trodden it was like concrete.

My delight at discovering that another puppy lived next door was to be short lived. He was of a similar age to me and for several weeks we were great buddies but suddenly his temperament altered, he became very aggressive and I acquired some very nasty scars. Four dogs lived on the opposite side and I enjoyed many hours innocently sitting by the chain-link fence watching them play together, until they too began to resent my vigil and fiercely attacked the fence tearing enormous holes through the wire. My Mum frequently had to patch up both the fence and me. She was terrified they may eat me alive if they ever broke through.

Aggression was not really my style but these experiences soon taught me that not all dogs were as tolerant as Soames and I must defend myself when necessary. Hoping a friendly romp was in store, I now observed caution when meeting strange dogs, I never made the first aggressive move but would quickly retaliate if war were declared. I very soon established and never forgot, which dogs in the neighbourhood were friendly and which were safest to avoid.

My Master and I vividly remember, when out walking together one Sunday morning, meeting an Old English Sheepdog of previous hostilities. In the ensuing struggle to separate us, I miscalculated and sunk one of my large fangs into an intervening hand which, unfortunately for both of us, happened to be my Master's. On the stark realization of what I had done I froze and humbly accepting the punishment administered returned home tail tightly clamped between my legs, meanwhile my Master headed hastily in the direction of the local hospital.

Chapter 5

I RARELY indulged in thieving but have to confess to a periodic lapse of willpower, like the large slab of butter that mysteriously vanished from a table set for a dinner party - and I wasn't even sick! Then I became overwhelmed by the powerful, almost magnetic attraction of large freshly baked fruitcakes. Lasting memories of my tea party in the garden with Aunty Dorothy inspired my Mum to attach me to the washing line on this occasion, making it evident that my participation was not required. I was deeply hurt but fortunately one of the guests took pity on me and engineered my release. Before his action could be questioned, I thundered across the garden like greased lightening, scooped up the cake whilst still in full flight and came to rest at the far end of the lawn where, held between my mighty paws I proceeded to devour my prize. Regretfully the opportunity to repeat this exercise came only once more as thereafter, preventative measures were always strictly enforced.

I was particularly partial to ham but never being officially included in my diet I had to resort to devious means. One day the succulent aroma drifting from a plate full of this sliced delicacy, left unguarded for just a few seconds, was certainly beyond my powers of resistance and well worth the inevitable reprimand. "Thunderpaws" they may well call me, but I could be extremely agile as I demonstrated on a family outing to Biggin Hill Airshow. We arrived with a packed lunch which included a large stack of delicious smelling ham sandwiches, clearly none were allocated to me so I decided to patiently bide my time. About mid-day sitting round a small table my family relaxed with their picnic. Luck was on my side when the unannounced and silent approach of four Tornado fighter jets suddenly created an ear piercing eruption as they passed directly overhead. Spontaneously everyone's astonished gaze was averted to the sky above, everyone except me that is, who's desire for those sandwiches left me no option, completely oblivious to the noise, this momentary distraction was all I needed to seize and consume the lot. Well, I was in disgrace yet again but at least I was satisfied in more ways than one, my stomach was full and I felt very proud when I overheard them praising my initiative and split second timing.

Sadly this total disregard for loud noises was not to last. A rather unpleasant experience occurred soon after in my own garden of all places, a teenage neighbour armed with an air-gun, targeted me from his bedroom window. Thereafter any sudden bangs would send me into a fit of nervous frenzy and this fear was further extended to include both thunder and fireworks. Living in the country, where farmers often used scare guns on their newly seeded crops, became a frightening ordeal, exaggerated by also living close to a garrison town where a firing range was in frequent operation and explosive experiments were regularly executed.

Butter wouldn't melt in my mouth!

Confined to the kitchen and all alone in the house, one such explosion caused absolute havoc, I frantically scratched open the kitchen door desperate for somewhere safe to hide. I thundered up the stairs and into the bathroom where the door fitted on rising-butts closed behind me. In my determined and demented attempt to escape, I then accidentally clipped the lock into position and there I had to remain trapped and terrified until someone returned home. My Mum duly arrived, confused by my absence, she dashed upstairs and soon realized where I was, but as the lock could only be released from the inside, my rescue was delayed even further whilst she quickly became proficient in the art of breaking and entering. She eventually appeared to my surprise, through the bathroom window, no mean feat I understand, since she was apparently scared of climbing ladders. By that time I was overcome by both mental and physical exhaustion and lay in a collapsed heap surrounded by the shredded remains of mats, towels, carpet and even the padded jacket once neatly fitted around the tank in the airing cupboard. Only the main fixtures in the bathroom had escaped my rampage, in fact you might easily be forgiven for assuming the explosion had actually occurred in that very room.

I seem to remember that an unexpected thunderstorm caused another similar incident but on this occasion the room resembled the scene of a rather brutal murder. Again I had managed to escape from the kitchen but this time headed for a bedroom newly fitted with a beautiful pink shag-pile carpet. I truly believed that if I could only bury myself under that everything would be all right, so intense was my digging that I barely noticed the sharp teeth of the gripper rods securing the carpet edges. Not only was the carpet torn to shreds so too were the pads of my front paws. I'm sure the loss of all that blood should have warranted a transfusion!

My phobia really did produce genuine fear and it soon became essential that I was never left alone in such circumstances. November 5th became an annual nightmare, tranquillizers did little to ease my distress and it was only in my latter years that the problem resolved itself. I suppose looking on the positive side there had to be at least one advantage to becoming deaf.

Chapter 6

I WAS about eighteen months old when another attempt at furthering my education was booked in the form of training classes held in a local Church Hall. I was taken regularly once a week and began to look forward to this terribly social outing and even showed signs of improvement until about the fourth week. I was one of a dozen dogs, all obediently walking to heel one behind the other in a large circle, then the Instructor directed each of the handlers to give the "sit and stay" command. Once all the dogs, including me had successfully complied, our owners were asked to reverse slowly into the centre. Well, I utilized this unique opportunity to make the personal acquaintance of all the other dogs whilst uninhibited by their owner. Clearly my fun loving behaviour clashed seriously with the strict discipline required by the Instructor and when I repeatedly refused to conform, I was ultimately expelled on the grounds of being a bad influence on the rest of the class. Apart from the choke chain giving me an extremely sore neck, I achieved little benefit, but I'm sure my Mum certainly learned to fully appreciate the difficulties of exercising control over a terrier that simply adored being in trouble.

Talking of trouble, over the years I managed to accumulate an extremely fat medical file. Initially I eagerly attended my appointments with the Vet and preferred to announce my own arrival by jumping up and placing my large front paws on the desk. The surprised Receptionist then had no doubts at all about who had yet another appointment as her eyes met my cheery gaze. However this eagerness was to be short-lived, over the years, the large number of strange lumps, bumps, teeth, glands and warts requiring attention and the rather unpleasant experience of frequent anaesthetics soon altered my attitude. In fact, considerable force was then required to coax this now reluctant patient out of the car, let alone into the surgery.

I remember once when there was not a vacant kennel large enough for me to await an operation, it was suggested that I be left tied up to a radiator attached to the wall in the operating area. Absolving herself from the blame for any consequential mutilation to the plumbing, my Mum left me at the discretion of the Veterinary Nurse and on her return cowardly opted against making any further inquiries.

Then there was the morning I managed to injure a front paw whilst cavorting around the reservoir, I was found in a whimpering pitiful heap amongst the long grass. When my impractical plea to be carried home was ignored, despite excruciating pain I was coerced slowly back on three legs. The fuss I made led everyone, including the Vet, to automatically assume my paw must be badly broken until a subsequent x-ray proved that I had suffered no more than a severe sprain, nonetheless it was still extremely painful.

So frequent were my visits to the Vet that he soon became a family friend, which was rather fortuitous when in the evening one Sunday an unscheduled visit to his house became vital. One of my ears had dramatically transformed itself into a huge and extremely heavy bulbous sack. It was most uncomfortable and felt like a lead weight dragging my head to the ground. It transpired that I had burst a blood vessel, this had to be drained and necessitated a selection of buttons being sewn to my envelope shaped flap to keep it flat and shrivel free as it healed. It was really humiliating when people stared in amusement but at least I knew what to expect when a few months later exactly the same thing happened to the other ear.

The year the dreaded Parvo-virus hit Britain with a vengeance, many puppies and older dogs did not survive, this sadly included two of my friends. I need scarcely mention that I too contracted the disease but was one of the lucky ones, weight dropped off me and I was extremely ill for several days. I distinctly remember the worst part of my treatment involved the Vet having to slowly inject a thick fluid into my rump via a massive syringe. Ear-piecing howls fiercely registered my opinion of this procedure to the whole neighbourhood, but then back at home I enjoyed an abundance of loving care and copious doses of kaolin and morphine which all served to set me back on my paws in no time.

My well being was always of prime importance to my family and on one occasion their annual holiday abroad had to be cancelled on my behalf. My waterworks were the cause for concern this time, apart from the hygiene aspect, incontinence is not a pleasant experience and I was clearly embarrassed and distressed by my uncontrollable dribble. Being mid-way through a series of tests and to avoid any interruption, an alternative impromptu boating holiday on the river was arranged. This did give me an unscheduled opportunity to become Captain Brillo for a week, most days I could be seen sitting on the front hatch wearing a blue cap which seemed to delight the other holiday makers. Jumping on and off the boat was a skill quickly mastered and despite the hazards of negotiating all the locks, even I failed to ascertain whether or not I could actually swim. Exploring new territory each day we had some wonderful walks, usually culminating with refreshments at a local pub. I soon adjusted to life on board a boat and exhausted by all the fresh air was content to be left on guard during the evenings.

Captain Brillo

However I'm forgetting, the reason for this holiday was to enable early morning samples of my embarrassing problem to be collected, and sent by post to the Vet for analysis. Each morning when most normal people were still asleep my Mum, armed with a soup ladle, would follow me along the riverbank, the ladle was then accurately poised to catch the required specimen as I lifted my leg against the first tree. Oblivious to the importance of this exercise I usually clumsily managed to trip over the ladle upsetting most of its content in my haste to find the next lucky tree. Any bleary-eyed spectator unfortunate enough to witness all this probably immediately lost their appetite for the bacon and egg he or she may have been cooking for breakfast that morning. On our return home the final results of these tests were fairly inconclusive, but as a last resort an operation depriving me of my manhood did eventually solve the problem. Incidentally, I'm sure it was nothing personal, but soup was not included in my family's diet again for a very long time.

Chapter 7

THE timing of that operation was to alter my life in more ways than the obvious. Still sleepy from the anaesthetic, I was collected from the recovery room where only one other animal remained. He was a scared, scraggy but otherwise healthy, black cat of about eight years whose owner didn't want him any more and had asked for him to be put to sleep. I was not at all surprised he was unwanted but the Vet, who didn't share my biased view had taken pity on him and was searching for a suitable new home. He explained to my Mum that the cat had never lived indoors and could earn his keep controlling the mice population in our stable yard. Not convinced, she nevertheless promised to consider the idea, which I of course hated but was in no fit state to register my feelings.

Ten days later when I returned to have my stitches professionally removed, or at least those which I hadn't already eaten, the cat was still resident and looking even more forlorn and rejected. Without any consideration for me, my Mum relented and allowed the Vet to deliver him to our house the following day. He was given the name "Black-Jack", Blackie for short, and he quickly established a home for himself in the hay-shed and became a very affectionate and eternally grateful feline, he also proved to be a champion rat and mouse catcher. I seized every available opportunity to scare and chastise him if ever he ventured beyond the gate of the stable yard. Persistent as he was, I had no intention of relinquishing my superior position within the family.

So intent was I to ensure Blackie never trespassed on my territory that calamity struck one sunny afternoon when I spotted him daring to cross the far end of the garden, I just didn't notice poor innocent Grandma, who had the misfortune to be standing in my flight path. I merely brushed passed her, but at full speed it was sufficient to knock her off-balance, she fell awkwardly and was unfortunate enough to crack her wrist on the concrete path and badly injure her leg. My family was so ashamed of me, but dear Grandma always such a lovely kind and gentle lady, despite the pain and suffering my over-exuberance had caused, unreservedly continued to love me just the same.

It perhaps would not have been quite so bad had I not, a few years earlier, been the cause of Grandad breaking his leg in two places. I had stayed overnight with my Grandparents and the following morning had already had one walk, but being thoroughly spoilt, Grandad decided to take me out again before I went back home. On this ill-fated jaunt I was eager to meet other dogs also enjoying a stroll along the promenade, this notion however conflicted with Grandad's determined effort to prevent me from becoming so acquainted. Our difference of opinion concluded when my lead somehow entwined itself around his legs causing him to topple over, and my illogical interpretation of human behaviour prompted me to assume Grandad had actually sat down on the pavement to play with me. However, I soon sensed something awful had happened when he was unwilling and indeed unable to participate in a game. Several people appeared on the scene, someone dragged me away and we had to wait several minutes until a white van with blue flashing lights and noisy siren arrived. Two uniformed Ambulance Crew jumped out to attend to poor Grandad and take him to the hospital, meanwhile feeling very confused, I was escorted, tail between my legs again, back to Grandma's house by a kindly gentleman who had the awesome task of explaining what had happened.

Surprisingly enough Grandad too, was able to find forgiveness but after eight long weeks of a very hot summer with his leg in plaster, forgetting was a much harder task. I never deliberately intended any harm to come to anybody, but by now my reputation was in shreds. These two incidents were genuine accidents so it surely had to be a cruel twist of fate that somehow I was involved in both.

Chapter 8

I WAS taken for long walks each day and became extremely fit running round the fields. I loved disappearing amongst the golden corn during the summer months and periodically having to leap high above it to assess my whereabouts before haphazardly rustling off in some other direction. The moving corn was the only clue as to where I might possibly re-appear from amongst the extensive acreage.

A favourite walk of mine followed a footpath that led to a secluded reservoir. Its wide grassy banks, flanked on three sides by shrubs and woodland, offered a superb setting for the fishermen who spent many peaceful hours up there, well they did until I arrived on the scene to shatter the tranquillity. Most of them were very tolerant, even when I helped myself to their sandwiches together with a tasty mouthful of wriggling bait. However their patience usually expired when I insisted on splashing around in the water disturbing the fish and falsely activating the buzzers, then as I emerged I would shake myself violently to ensure everyone within close proximity ended up as wet and muddy as myself. My popularity diminished further in mid-summer when the water level was somewhat lower and I was obliged to wade through several feet of thick green, foul-smelling, stagnant sludge before actually reaching any water. My poor Mum seemed to spend a large portion of her time apologizing on my behalf, but I simply adored people and couldn't resist being sociable even if my enthusiastic greeting was not always reciprocated.

Maybe partial retribution was paid for my misconduct when one day up on the reservoir my inquisitiveness lured me towards a broken length of fishing line left abandoned in the long grass. The lead weight was still attached to the tangled twine and a savage barbed hook that somehow became embedded through my right eyelid. Fortunately it had narrowly missed my eye but the weight was dragging down that side of my face, so as you can imagine I was in a very distressed state until my Mum came to the rescue and carefully succeeded in removing the offensive weapon.

Then some years later, at this same location, a far more serious incident occurred. It had been snowing very heavily the previous week, my exercise had been somewhat curtailed but after the weekend access to the reservoir was once again possible. I bounded off in delight, jumping the snow filled ditches and throwing myself into the sweeping drifts. Obviously the adverse weather conditions were not conducive to fishing so the place was deserted even rather spooky with an abundance of huge icicles suspended on the overhanging trees. The reservoir was frozen with ice several inches thick and that day I discovered a whole range of exciting new activities, skating being the first.

The Reservoir,
I prefer to remember it in summer!

Swimming soon became the second, I had traversed about fifteen feet across the frozen surface when suddenly the ice began to crack beneath my paws, I plunged through a hole about two feet in diameter and was submerged in ice cold water. I swam round and round desperately trying to haul myself out, but the edges were solid and so very slippery. My Mum was panic struck, talking to me all the time she tried to reach me but the ice began to crack under her weight filling her wellington boots with freezing water. All my efforts were hopeless, overcome by fear, which was something I had never before experienced, I could not understand why my Mum was now running away from me across the snow clad field. Didn't she realize I desperately wanted to join her but couldn't, and why should she want to abandon me at a time like this when I needed her most and was so helpless? Numb with cold I was tiring quickly sad and desolate I began to cry sorrowfully, how I longed now to be back home on my nice warm bed. As I grew colder and weaker, I miraculously summoned enough strength to cleverly wedge my front legs at right angles across the ice thus keeping at least my head above the water, then motionless, I resigned myself to the likelihood of literally freezing to death.

Suddenly my despair was lifted, two men appeared obviously aware of my predicament. I watched hopefully as they hastily wrenched some wooden tree stakes out of the ground, tied them to long lengths of string and by throwing them towards me frantically tried to smash a channel through the ice. Time was running out for me and their task was made more difficult when the string kept breaking, unable to retrieve the stakes, precious time was wasted as my concerned rescuers hurriedly searched for more. Closer and closer they hurled them towards me, still clinging to the ice I was absolutely petrified by this time, I even thought they were now trying to hit me and there I was totally unable to do anything about it. Then my Mum re-appeared, just as the last section of ice gave way. Instinctively, I mustered up sufficient energy to doggy-paddle along the channel of broken ice to the bank where I finally collapsed in a frozen, exhausted heap. I had been in the water for over forty minutes!

My Mum was eternally grateful to those two kind workmen who had saved me she had apparently seen them on her way to telephone for help. As she wrapped me up in her own warm coat a team of Firemen arrived on the scene complete with ladders and ropes. Although too late for my actual rescue, I did welcome a lift home. They gently carried my cold and shivering wet body to the warm cabin of the fire engine. The pristine appearance of that cabin slowly began to disintegrate as the balls of ice, frozen to my fur, thawed into pools of muddy water during the short journey home. I must confess to being too exhausted to fully appreciate the privilege of a ride in a real fire engine, an opportunity not experienced by many other dogs I'm sure. This was a great shame because my only other claim to an unconventional ride was in a substantially inferior vehicle, a milk float, which I briefly hi-jacked one day much to the dismay of the poor milkman who seemed too scared to push me out!

Nevertheless my survival from the reservoir was truly remarkable, it was a great blessing that my haircut scheduled for the previous week had been postponed, for without the protective insulation of a thick, woolly and oily coat I probably would not have made it. The Vet was amazed at my stamina and said a human would only have lasted about half the time in such appalling conditions. He treated me for shock and boosted my tired muscles with a hefty steroid injection. Sincerely glad to be warm and dry in the safety of my own home I slept for the next twenty four hours on my comfortable bean bag bed which had long replaced the wicker basket of my puppy days. Apart from losing two stone in weight I suffered no other ill effects, in fact I bounced back to being my normal self two days later when it all seemed like a very bad dream.

In my latter years when almost blind, falling into a neighbour's fishpond, seemed a tame experience after that classic ordeal, but what will always remain a mystery to me is why did I have the misfortune to find the only patch of thin ice on the whole reservoir?

Chapter 9

FORTUNATELY for the mental sanity of my family, incidents on that scale were rare, my own sanity however was questionable. It could be argued that maybe I was trying to knock some sense into myself when I frequently charged up the garden only coming to an abrupt halt when I collided with the brick wall. I suppose it could be interpreted as plain stupidity, but either way I would pick myself up without so much as a flinch or yelp and go to search for the next spot of bother.

Having deferred maturity until my teenage years and making full use of my exuberant vitality, I was able to astound my family on countless occasions throughout my extended puppy-hood, with my relentless ability to magnetically attract trouble of all degrees. I was blessed with an almost magical charm that endeared me to most people who, unless they had a general dislike of all dogs, were led to believe that nearly all my misdemeanours were excusable.

I remember the time I was merely flavour testing the wrapping paper of a newly repaired sandwich maker when it seemingly just happened to jump off the table all by itself and never worked again. Another day a workman was spotted sneaking off to the village shop, when my Mum was convinced she had seen him arrive that morning with a very full sandwich box. I cannot accurately recall now, whether I had raided it before or after the large paw-prints mysteriously appeared in the beautiful smooth concrete he had just painstakingly laid!

Delving into handbags was one of my favourite occupations I was intrigued by the huge variety of items I could reveal, often to the consternation of its owner. Inquisitive by nature, I couldn't resist investigating the contents of those flip-top rubbish bins generally found in a kitchen, but proving my innocence was always difficult when caught wearing the inverted lid clamped securely around my neck. Talking of rubbish makes me remember the fun I often had pouncing on the neat pile of floor sweepings found awaiting the arrival of a dustpan and brush. Once suitably dispersed, I would try to make myself scarce but the copious amount of fluff and dust stuck to my large wet nose invariably made me the most likely culprit. I must tell you, my Mum also found the dustpan and brush a useful piece of equipment when returning to the garden, the numerous hedgehogs I befriended. Oblivious to their prickly coats, I liked to gently carry them indoors and invite them to share my bed. I was then left wondering why, once any stray quills had been removed from around my mouth, it seemed essential to cover me with flea spray, when I made it quite clear that I detested aerosols. The noise distinctly reminded me of that first unpleasant encounter I had with a bicycle!

I was a very sociable fellow and found it very hurtful to hear my family comment on how I would probably welcome a burglar in the middle of the night as an unexpected playmate. It cast doubt on my ability to be a true guard dog, when I happened to know that an unknown quantity of my stature would surely be enough to deter any intruder.

Visitors however, were always greeted with enthusiasm particularly if they came to stay overnight, it seemed only courteous to help unpack their suitcase. I remember one such guest, who likewise well remembers me, whose beard was a source of considerable interest and focus of my attention throughout his stay. Never before had I encountered a hairy-faced human and I wasn't at all sure whether to expect him to speak or bark!

Predictable and repetitive behaviour I classified as boring and therefore could not understand why my Mum's heart sank when soon after, a bearded policeman arrived on the doorstep one sunny afternoon. Her concern was quite unfounded I hardly noticed his beard as he was wearing a most extraordinary and much more appealing thing on his head. I actually was the cause of his visit, but it was not what you may be thinking, for once I was totally innocent as I had found some money whilst out walking earlier in the day. Having made my acquaintance I think the Constable rather liked me at that stage. He was then ushered into the lounge where he removed his helmet before sitting down to take arduous notes, whilst so engrossed I nonchalantly strolled passed his chair and ventured out into the garden via the open patio doors. It was some time before anyone noticed that on the way through I had discreetly collected the helmet and was lying in the middle of the lawn proudly investigating my latest treasure. My Mum was aghast with horror when she realized and of course I had to surrender it immediately but totally unabashed I quietly returned to the lawn this time with his gloves. Luckily the damage was minimal before they too were retrieved and I successfully evaded instant arrest. That escape reminds me of my shoplifting incident that began and ended in a large department store in the days before "No Dogs Allowed" notices were prominently displayed on every shop door.

It was quite an embarrassing experience I believe firstly I, accidentally of course, overturned a stand spread with ladies make-up of all descriptions, there were lipsticks, bottles of nail varnish and little pots of this and that rolling under the counters and around the other customer's feet. We were making a hasty exit when I hesitated briefly to argue with a tub of feather dusters that certainly looked quite ferocious and whilst being dragged away from those, I unobtrusively stole the dark curly wig from a now bald-headed plaster model. Once my Mum discovered what I had done, I was quickly escorted back to the store where she offered sincere apologies to an assistant who seemed to have a distinct sense of humour failure. She severely reprimanded us both as she re-instated the model to her former, but now rather soggy, glory. Further down the road I expressed my extreme disapproval of being tethered outside a branch of a large Supermarket, by howling loudly for the whole duration of my Mum's absence. I expect this enhanced her concentration on the shopping she was trying to do, being continually reminded that no one could possibly have stolen me.

I can only assume shopping with me was not to be recommended as I wasn't taken again, and I think the closest I ever came, was a visit to an

Antique Fair one Sunday afternoon. Although I didn't actually put a paw out of place my arrival, was greeted with a great deal of apprehension by all of the stand-holders. It wasn't my fault that my nose just happened to be exactly the same height as their stalls laden with a vast variety of delicate "objects d'art". To the relief of all concerned, tight control ensured this excursion passed without any mishap.

Chapter 10

FOR some obscure reason I never stayed with my Grandparents again but I did enjoy an annual holiday in some kennels situated some forty miles from home. As my happiness was of paramount importance, an inspection of all the local boarding kennels was made on my behalf before finding one suitable. Some had rather cramped living quarters, particularly for a large dog like myself, some were overcrowded, other ones were hygienically unsuitable and the owners of two actually refused to even allow my Mum to see where I was to stay during my vacation.

A very nice family owned the kennel finally selected and it also happened to be a poultry farm, this obviously proved to be additional bonus for the residents. Only a few dogs were boarded and we were all tended in the same meticulous manner as their own show dogs which the proprietor also bred. I was groomed regularly and each day enjoyed the freedom of the enormous runs. Every year I eagerly returned for I knew fresh chicken or turkey was always on the menu. Many years of patronage made me a firm favourite with this family who always greeted me warmly on my arrival, my Mum was always reluctant to leave me behind and tried to hide her sadness as I was led away to my kennel, tail held high and happily wagging. Only once was I made to feel a little uneasy.

I had been thoroughly groomed before the journey. My bag of toys and "goodboy" biscuits was being loaded into the car when it became imperative for me to investigate the source of a strong odour drifting in from the garden. Anyway I also had to say goodbye to the gardener who was certainly going to miss my help in the forthcoming weeks. He was working hard that particular day fertilizing the lawn with a compound of dried blood and bone meal. The sack of mixture was easy to locate, I threw myself headfirst into it, eating huge mouthfuls as I burrowed and when I finally surfaced my whole head was stained bright orange with teeth to match. Apparently by human standards the stench was horrendous and little improved by a very necessary hot soapy facial scrub and teeth scouring session which promptly followed. Repentant as I was, being confined with me in the car for the next forty-five minutes, even with all the windows open, did little to improve my popularity.

However, albeit accidentally, one day my Mum had cause to be very thankful for one of my messy exploits. Walking through the woods on the far side of the reservoir, we sometimes returned home via the road. There was a large white gate at the end of the track situated on the corner of a very sharp bend. It was here that I was usually reunited with my lead, though I must confess to occasions when I backed-tracked home alone, I could never comprehend why my Mum was so irate when she arrived much later to find me sitting safely on the doorstep waiting for her. On this particular day, I had been rummaging through the undergrowth in the woods and had emerged with thousands upon thousands of little round burrs embedded throughout my curly coat. We went through the gate, where my Mum, in despair of my appearance, hesitated for a few moments to briskly remove several hundred. It was in those few seconds a speeding lunatic driver screeched round the sharp bend, narrowly missing the ditch as his car mounted the grass verge where we almost certainly would have been walking had I not provided my Mum with this little task. The next time however, I was not so fortunate, our front driveway has two exits bordered on each side by a very wide and tall laurel hedge obscuring a good view of the road. My family was momentarily distracted as they bade farewell to some visitors, when on the far side of the road one of my girlfriends happened to be passing the other exit and I bolted across to see her. All I can remember now is a loud bang followed by silence, broken only by my Mum's loud scream as she rushed out expecting the worst. A very distressed driver sat ashen faced shaking in his now stationary car, he had bowled me over as I collided with his front wheel. Feeling slightly giddy and bruised, I picked myself up, gave a hearty shake and trotted coolly back indoors, leaving my relieved family to offer sympathy and an appropriate apology to the innocent victim of my carelessness. Maybe there is some truth after all in the saying "Where there's no sense there's no feeling".

I loved being with my Mum and would stay by the side-gate, sometimes for several hours, patiently awaiting her return from exercising the horses, ready to greet them enthusiastically when they eventually came home. I did have enough sense however, to only need one lesson when I tried to nip the heels of the horses as they walked down the garden path. When I narrowly evaded a metal shod hoof aimed with a force capable of rearranging my handsome face, I resorted instead to frantic barking from a safe distance. The only other useful thing the horses ever taught me was how to graze, I studied the art carefully, practiced regularly and found the fine Cumberland turf of the lawn particularly appetizing, even if the roots were a little tough!

Waiting for my Mum

Chapter 11

WHEN I was four years old my Mum disappeared for a few days, I knew something exciting was happening but didn't fully understand what, until she came home carrying a curious bundle in her arms, all snugly wrapped up in a soft pink shawl. I was told to be very, very gentle as I eagerly inspected this new addition to our family. Her name was Suzannah and there was no reason for me to feel at all jealous, as my Mum insisted the many visitors, who called during the next few days, acknowledged me first, before being allowed to enthuse over the new baby. I delighted in all the attention and was overwhelmed with an enormous sense of responsibility, as I desperately wanted to become her friend and adored sitting for hours close to the pram, protecting our new little baby whenever she was asleep in the garden.

As her self-appointed guardian it was appropriate that several months later my name, or at least her version of it, was the first word she uttered, she would point a tiny finger at me, in her unique upside down manner, excitedly repeating "Bree Bree". I became well loved amongst her little friends as she grew up and enjoyed participating in her annual birthday party. Helping to unwrap someone else's presents was almost as much fun as opening my own, and then enthusiastically shredding the wrapping paper into confetti sized pieces certainly enhanced the appearance of the lounge.

Having achieved front passenger seat status following Suzannah's birth, my manners in the car improved enormously. My solid frame filled the entire seat, wedged against the back I would sit bolt upright and soon learned to lean into the bends, looking and feeling terribly important as I nonchalantly surveyed the outside world. This stance usually raised a few smiles especially when we pulled up alongside other vehicles at traffic lights. I was regularly chauffeur-driven to collect Suzannah from school. I must admit many of her tiny friends were at first daunted by my size but soon came to realize I was a playful but very gentle giant.

In my protective capacity I remember becoming very agitated and concerned when one day I saw my Mum repeatedly thumping Suzannah, quite hard on her back as she lay head down across a footstool. I anxiously tried to intervene only to be harshly scolded and pushed away. Nobody had bothered to explain some physiotherapy was being administered but in hindsight, I suppose I should have realized the patient was not protesting.

My excellent singing voice, though not highly rated by the rest of the family, was one of my party-pieces and was usually precipitated by any high-pitched sound. I would often render a spooky choral serenade in the still of the night, doubtless induced by one of my more than vivid dreams. I could continue a repertoire of throaty howls in various pitches for several minutes delivered with such enthusiasm that my front legs would often leave the ground as I hit the highest notes. Whenever Suzannah played her recorder I always liked to perform in unison, but as nobody else seemed to appreciate the musical merit of our duet I was usually removed from the room fairly promptly. Talking in my sleep was another of my vocal talents often accompanied by galloping or quivering legs as I bounded about in my dreams. I would maintain quite a flowing conversation of contented doggy grunts in response to any show of affection and perhaps I shouldn't admit it, but I adored an occasional cuddle. However I could equally register disapproval in no uncertain terms, by emitting forceful consecutive groans of self-pity, if sent to my bed having reluctantly conceded to discipline.

Dare I now relate what was probably the most shameful performance of my whole life? It was a beautiful mid-summer evening and Grannie and Poppa, my other Grandparents, had come to baby-sit. As they waved goodbye to my Mum and Dad, I decided to take a solitary stroll. Poppa just spotted my tail disappearing through the front hedge, I chose to ignore his call knowing he was bound to follow me anyway. As I trotted round the bend, I met Oscar, a rather stout Jack Russell Terrier who lived at the corner house. For years he had irritated me intensely by yapping provocatively whenever I walked past, but always being on the lead I had never been able to retaliate. Today was different, for the first time ever I was at liberty to chase him. His family was sitting outside on their raised patio, relaxing with some friends and enjoying the last of the evening sun, around a table clustered with bottles and drinks in cut crystal glasses. Oscar realizing his mistake fled for cover with me in hot pursuit. Within seconds the tranquillity of the evening was shattered, the table overturned on impact as I bowled into little Oscar. I had only intended to scare him a little, but as my jaws encased his stout little body, my sharp canine fangs pierced his sides and I was then unable to open my mouth wide enough to let go. Shaking my head violently, trying to release him, I ran through the house as Oscar's blood started to trickle and sprayed over the furniture, walls and white lounge carpet.

A very dismayed Poppa arrived on the scene quite unable to comprehend how so much damage could have been done in so short a time. Try to imagine what beheld him, broken glasses, spilled drinks, hysterical screams, splattered blood and somebody trying to prize open my mouth to rescue poor terrified little Oscar now squealing loudly. He incidentally had to spend the night in intensive care suffering from shock and deep puncture wounds that required several stitches and it took a long time for him to recuperate. I really did have to keep a very low profile after that dreadful episode, well at least until Oscar came off the danger list. Quite rightly everyone's sympathy rested with him whose punishment far outweighed his petty crime of yapping.

Fortunately for everyone and especially me he did make a full recovery. Though unfortunately for my family, their Insurance Company declined to accept any liability for the damage caused as Oscar's garden had no fence around it. They stated that dogs will be dogs and negligence could not be proved if there was no restraining boundary. Nevertheless, my mortified family felt honour bound to settle the resulting bills.

Chapter 12

NO sooner had I resigned myself to Blackjack's presence than my Mum found an abandoned kitten cowering in a nearby ditch. A sad little ginger waif only about six weeks old, he was undernourished, covered in ticks and fleas and sneezing his tiny head off. Sparing no thought whatsoever for me he was carefully carried to the safe domain of Blackie's stable-yard. Blackie took an instant shine to him and nominated himself as his personal defender. I actually thought he was being slightly over-protective when he forbade me to even look, but four months later an opportunity arose for me to introduce myself. The kitten had been tenderly nursed and fed back to good health and grown considerably. I cannot begin to imagine how he acquired his name but Mini-Whiskers, seeking to broaden his own horizons, inquisitively ventured through the gate one day. Overtly keen to meet him, I failed to notice Blackie's watchful eye until he pounced on me, Mini-Whiskers vanished amidst a scurry of spiteful hissing and spitting. I was so dumbfounded, I didn't think to retaliate until Blackie, remembering his charge, made a sudden retreat to search for Mini-Whiskers and as he slid under the gate I dived after him just in time to grasp a mouthful of tail.

No, I did not bite it off completely, but the wound I inflicted became so infected, the Vet had to amputate several inches leaving a short stub as a permanent reminder of yet one more of my shameful misdemeanours. Brave Blackie proudly exhibited his honourable battle scar and became a living hero. Mini-Whiskers remained rather shy and withdrawn. He would curiously vanish whenever strangers appeared but loved the attention bestowed upon him by Blackie, his faithful guardian and friend who pinned him down, sometimes several times a day, for a thorough wash.

For several years Blackie was content to dwell in the feed shed snuggling up with Mini-Whiskers on cold winter nights in a straw filled box, dutifully sharing the rat and mouse patrol until, for undisclosed reasons Blackie suddenly had illusions of grandeur and decided he wanted to be a house-cat. My Mum often said everyone should have ambition so I had to assume that also included mere cats! I was now getting on in years and it became an uphill struggle to conserve the house as a cat-free zone. Ultimately I was forced to relent and permit

Blackie to sit on one of the chairs in the kitchen, an advantage point from which he could smack me sharply on the nose, often drawing blood, when I overdid the chastising. A mutual respect for one another was gradually established.

Blackie & Minnie Whiskers keeping each other warm

I evaded old age for a very long time and became a teenage puppy. I celebrated my birthdays and each Christmas with piles of presents and cards, all unwrapped by myself of course. Grandma's gift was always a squeaky toy of invaluable use when my Dad was watching sport on the television, of which I was very jealous and any kind of attention was surely preferable to none. Without actually maturing, old age inevitably enveloped me though certain privileges helped ease the reality, like the occasional nap on the sofa and being allowed to help myself to those viscous Bonio biscuits living in the kitchen cupboard. Table manners became almost non-existent as I persistently scrounged for food at mealtimes. At fourteen there was not a grey hair on my jet-black back, my appearance was spoilt only by some nasty ugly warts which multiplied on my eyelids, they often bled and required regular bathing and soothing ointment was needed to allay the discomfort. My Mum had decided I was too old to risk the anaesthetic that would be required to remove them. The only way I could alleviate the irritation myself without feeling any pain, was to massage my head gently along the carpet pile but even that made them bleed, and in no way did it improve the appearance of the carpet.

My eyes began to sink further into my skull as cataracts obscured my vision, bumping into things was now a frequent occurrence and I no longer needed to pretend to be deaf! I learned to rely on whoever took me out to be my ears and eyes, besides by now I really couldn't go very far anyway. Off the lead I quickly became disorientated, looking helplessly lost I would stand rigid in the middle of a field, tail clamped firmly between my legs until my Mum came to the rescue, the relief was enormous as she gave me a reassuring hug. Having always been so fit and strong it was hard to cope with the faulty mechanics of my back legs that now felt as if they were made of wood.

No expense was spared ensuring my declining years were made as comfortable as possible. A new much larger bed, which my Mum manufactured especially for me, was heavily padded with polystyrene beads. In my younger days I'm sure I could have effected a fairly impressive explosion in the kitchen but now it took several hesitant approaches before I felt secure enough to even lie down on it, let alone fall asleep. I was disconcerted by the funny crunchy noises it made as I wobbled over its generous square footage. Restricted activity in my latter years made me susceptible to the cold, my joints were particularly vulnerable and a heater was considerately left on overnight. My Mum made me a special fleecy lined coat for outdoor use, I concluded Dad disapproved as I noticed he rarely took me out anymore. Although I slept deeply nearly all the time and became completely deaf, it was uncanny how I knew when the biscuit tin went silently into the lounge. The considerable effort required to stagger from the kitchen was usually well rewarded before I slumped down in front of the blazing log fire onto the thick hearth-rug, which I had personally selected for comfort, from several samples brought home some years earlier.

Blazing log fire – Bliss!

I had always loved being out in the fresh air and enjoyed the secure familiarity of my garden more than ever. I would often sit in the middle of the lawn, head held high, taking in the air, (as every Airedale should) and listen to the birds twittering. Indoors I would lie with my back clamped close to the patio window soaking up the sun, now with the energy to only dream of the excavations I used to dig and the paths I trampled around the flower boarders. In the cool of the long summer evenings I could occasionally muster the willpower and effort needed to participate in a game of short tennis if it was being played on the lawn. Pinching the ball was not beyond my capabilities but I found acting as referee far less energetic and I even condescended to allow both the cats to watch.

I appreciated the benefit of more car outings finding them a less strenuous way of covering ground than proper walks, the prospects of which were generally more exciting than the actuality. Nowadays I had even lost my former zest to argue with other dogs and adopted the more subdued art of menacing oblivion this worked particularly well with my Grandparent's poodle who was easily antagonized. Let me explain, I would focus singularly undivided attention upon one of my squeaky toys, then secretly daring him to steal it, would pretend not to notice him yapping and barking as he ran frenzied circles around me. I was not satisfied until he was in trouble for making too much noise. Similar tantalizing tactics were employed for the dog next door, we had several apple trees in the garden and when they were heavily laden with rosy fruit there was obviously a plentiful supply of fallings. I would then deliberately tease him by lying close to the dividing chain-linked fence, enthusiastically munching a delicious juicy sample whilst he looked on enviously.

Tomatoes were the only food I found truly distasteful but that didn't stop me picking them. If it was not the flavour that attracted me, then what proved so irresistible must have been the peculiar squirting sensation of pips and juice oozing through the holes, as my long sharp canine teeth pierced the rather tough skin of a plump ripened fruit found growing in the garden. Whilst on the subject of food, I simply adored carrots and enthusiastically helped unpack the weekly shopping in the hope of finding some and couldn't believe my luck the day I found an entire sack in the horse's feed shed. I managed to drag this onto the lawn, whereupon I laid down and munched away to my hearts content, but it wasn't long before someone came to find out what was keeping me so busy.

Chapter 13

MY life-threatening rescue from the reservoir may have been more newsworthy, but my real claim to fame took nearly fourteen years to accomplish. It was however, in similar freezing February weather conditions when I legitimately had my name broadcast over the radio and I appeared, albeit fleetingly, on the main BBC Television News.

It had snowed heavily the previous day and had continued throughout the night. The next morning, it was still snowing when my family and a large group of neighbours invaded my garden and set about a most curious task, it kept them and me entertained until dusk. They laboriously manufactured large blocks of packed snow, which were transported from around the garden by sledge and then assembled to build a gigantic igloo. I couldn't possibly resist being involved in such activity and the children enjoyed giving me sledge rides on the empty return journeys.

When finished the igloo stood about eight feet high and the walls were nine inches thick, it was incredibly warm in there with room for forty people and me of course. Access was via a short low snow tunnel through which I could freely pass to inspect the progress, unlike everyone else who had to crawl in on their hands and knees. News of this construction quickly spread and a television crew arrived the next day to film my Mum tossing a pancake. A perfectly normal thing to do on Shrove Tuesday I understand but I gather, not usually executed inside an igloo! To this day, only I know for certain, whether the accurate timing of my little stroll past the camera just as it was filming was purely coincidental.

Helping the Cameraman

Later the same day a local radio reporter also visited. He interviewed Suzannah, who, when asked what her pets thought of the igloo, said, and I quote, "Blackie, our cat was frightened of it and ran out but our dog, "Brillo", just wandered about and then cocked his leg up against the inside wall". Then, asked if it had melted the snow, she giggled and replied, "No, but it did send it a funny colour!" Frankly, I thought the all-white finish looked a bit clinical!

I paid dearly for my brief encounter with fame, several days later it became apparent that I had caught a chill being outside in the snow for too long. This aggravated a painless but hard swelling which had been in my throat for a couple of years. My Vet had previously advised against an operation to remove the growth as the risks were far too great, but suddenly it became even more enlarged and began to impede my breathing which became very laboured, my heart was racing and I was reluctant to move at all. I was given antibiotics and other drugs to help relieve the discomfort and was allowed to remain in the lounge night and day. My Mum was terribly anxious she even slept downstairs on the sofa for three nights and I found it very reassuring to know she was there. I could only manage minute quantities of soft food and only then if the bowl was placed on a low stool, as the lump not only prevented me being able to swallow properly but the ability to lower my head was also severely restricted.

When, three days later, there was no sign of improvement consent was reluctantly given for the anaesthetic needed for further investigation. I was starved and denied water in readiness for the operation scheduled for the following day. I could sense my Mum was very distressed, she fussed over me and had a particularly restless night. Imagine her surprise, when she woke up the next morning to find me happily playing with one of my squeaky toys. Overjoyed, the operation was quickly postponed and an appointment made instead to review my recovery, which had progressed well by the time I actually saw the Vet. The lump had reduced to its normal size and the other symptoms slowly vanished. Feeling as well as I did and bored by the Vet's detailed advice on precautionary measures to prohibit a possible relapse, I unobtrusively slipped out of the surgery to meet and cheer-up the other sick patients in the waiting-room still awaiting their turn.

After that scare I enjoyed being more spoilt than ever, my meals thereafter were always comprised of soft food and served at a more convenient height, even my night-time biscuits were dunked in cocoa for extra safety. Each new day was considered a bonus and in the late spring a promise was fulfilled to re-visit the home where I was born. Candy, my real Mum was no longer there but another lady Airedale showed me round the garden. Distant, almost dreamlike, memories came flooding back to me of playful times with brothers and sisters, it was also encouraging to hear that one of my brothers was still living in the village.

That year being so docile now and considered too old to stay at the kennels, I was taken away with my family to Norfolk, they went there to spend a few days in a country cottage belonging to some friends. My bed was packed and I spread myself across the back seat of the car, leaving little room for Suzannah whose knees made an excellent headrest. It was lovely being included and I was impeccably behaved throughout my stay in the cottage and slept soundly on my bed placed at the bottom of the stairs each night. As the weather was kind it really didn't matter that I was confined to the garden for meals, as gulping sloppy food was a very messy business. We visited several delightful village pubs where I was much admired and complimented on my good manners. I wished I was younger but still enjoyed superb walks through forests and parks and one exhilarating trek along the cliffs, of course frequent rest periods were compulsory to allow my batteries to be re-charged. On this holiday an experience I could have well done without after fourteen years, was meeting my very first goat on a visit to a local farm. He was not much larger than me but a most unpleasant little character, he insisted on following me around all day and butting me with his horrid little horns.

Back home I quietly lazed my way through the rest of the summer, no longer confined to the kitchen when alone, I had earned the freedom of the house which I shared with Blackie who had patiently persevered in his effort to become a true house-cat. When a cat-flap was fitted to the back door as autumn fell, he knew that he had finally realized his dream and I was mostly too tired to argue. Poor Blackie was about fifteen years old by now, he had few teeth left, half a tail and only one of his eyes worked, that incidentally was no fault of mine. I'm told he also had trouble with his liver as he became extremely thin and consequently began to feel the cold. In a quaint and respectful way we grew very close, but sadly Blackie only enjoyed full house-cat status for a few weeks. Old age suddenly overtook him, having achieved his ambition, he lost the will to live and fell very, very sick. Inexplicably, after all these years, it was my company that he sought in his last few days and I was happy to allow him to snuggle up with me on my bed. It was my privilege to give him the warmth and comfort he needed on his final nights.

I'm feeling so very tired myself now and sad at losing my new friend. My Mum understands and if you don't mind, I'll let her continue........

Chapter 14

BY now Brillo was fourteen and a half years old. Christmas was drawing near and I told Suzannah he was going to ask Father Christmas for some new back legs, as his old ones were too stiff and worn out and wouldn't be strong enough to take him all the way to heaven when the time came. "Don't be silly Mummy," she promptly replied, "When Brillo dies, he won't need them because Jesus will come and carry him there in his arms."

Sadly Brillo never made Christmas that year. Perhaps on those two last nights, he and Blackie shared a secret beyond all human comprehension. He had behaved very strangely the day dear gentle Blackie died and it was the very next morning that our beloved Brillo followed in a way which, in true Brillo style, had to be as dramatic as the rest of his life.

The swelling in his throat suddenly enlarged again but what exactly happened, I guess we will never know, suffice it to say Brillo suffered a massive allergic re-action to an antibiotic and anti-inflammatory injection administered by the Vet earlier that day. If the car had been a jet airplane I doubt the hair-raising journey back to see the Vet could possibly have been any quicker. Then from somewhere I found the strength to carry him, now gasping loudly for breath, from the car straight through the crowded waiting room and into the surgery.

The Vet made a desperate and drastic emergency attempt to save Brillo. I stayed with him throughout, watching in stunned silence, but sorrowfully the Vet's efforts were all in vain. Numbed by the realization of what had just happened, yet grateful Brillo's suffering was not prolonged, I was absolutely devastated and tearfully drove him home to his final resting-place. Dear brave Brillo, he must have wondered during his last half-hour on this earth what was happening to him, but I thanked God that at least I had the privilege to be there, to do everything possible for him and he had not died all alone. It was a horrendously tragic end for such a boisterous, demanding, tough, yet most lovable roguish fellow, he really wasn't a naughty dog he just oozed so much character. His memory will stay with us always, indeed, how could we ever forget when others still frequently reminisce and say, "I remember when......."

EPILOGUE

BRILLO and Blackie now rest in peace, side by side in a shaded part of the garden they both loved so much. On a headstone they share these words....

Two Dear Friends
Blackie (1/12/1991) and Brillo (2/12/1991)

These two little bodies lie herein
Their souls have gone to heaven
Ever loving and forgiving
Contented with their humble living
They asked so little yet gave so much
Just a few kind words and gentle touch

Do animals have souls? If they have been truly loved, I think they do, for when they die they certainly take a part of you with them.

You may be wondering what happened to Mini-Whiskers, well, he had always been very shy and nervous of coming into the house, but Blackie had paved the way. He was desolate without his friend and plucked up the courage to use the cat flap. He would often be seen visiting their little graveyard, which he still does today.

We shared the pain of grief together and spent many hours consoling one another, both having lost a very best friend.

Printed in the United Kingdom
by Lightning Source UK Ltd.
109075UKS00001B/298-411